The Night the Thames Went Silent

*Inside the Marchioness Disaster:
London's Forgotten River Tragedy and
the Fight for Justice*

Richard B. Wray

Copyright

© 2025 Richard B. Wray. All rights reserved. No part of this publication may be reproduced, stored in a retrieval system, or transmitted in any form or by any means—electronic, mechanical, photocopying, recording, or otherwise—without the prior written permission of the author, except in the case of brief quotations used in critical articles or reviews.

Disclaimer

This book is based on real events surrounding the Marchioness disaster. Every effort has been made to ensure accuracy through publicly available records, verified testimonies, and credible sources. However, some dialogues, internal thoughts, and descriptive scenes have been reconstructed for narrative flow and reader engagement.

This book does not intend to defame, harm, or misrepresent any individual or organization. Any errors or omissions are unintentional. Readers are encouraged to consult official reports and archives for detailed legal and investigative records.

Dedication

To the fifty-one souls who never came home that night—
Your memory flows with the Thames, eternal and unforgotten.
And to the families, survivors, and silent heroes who carry the weight of those dark waters—
This book is for you.

Acknowledgments

Writing about the Marchioness disaster has been both a responsibility and a privilege. This book would not have been possible without the courage of survivors, the persistence of families, and the tireless efforts of those who documented the truth when the world moved on.

Special thanks to investigative journalists, researchers, and archivists whose work shed light on what might have remained buried. I also wish to acknowledge the emergency responders and divers whose bravery deserves to be remembered just as much as the lives they tried to save.

Finally, heartfelt gratitude to my readers—your curiosity and empathy keep stories like this alive, ensuring history never fades into silence.

Contents

Prologue

    A Night on the Thames

Chapter 1

    The Boats and Their Captains

Chapter 2

    Down the River: Early Hours

Chapter 3

    The Collision

Chapter 4

    Plunged into Darkness

Chapter 5

    Rescue and Chaos

Chapter 6

    Aftermath and Mourning

Chapter 7

Investigations Begin

Chapter 8

　　Trials and Legal Battles

Chapter 9

　　Public Inquiry and Report

Chapter 10

　　The Unanswered Questions

Chapter 11

　　The Voices We Almost Forgot

Chapter 12

　　Echoes Through Time

Epilogue

　　The Night That Changed the River

Quick Memory Challenge

Author's Note

The Marchioness disaster is not just a headline from the past—it is a haunting reminder of how quickly celebration can turn to tragedy. When I first began researching this event, I was struck by the silence surrounding it compared to its magnitude. Fifty-one lives lost on a summer night in the heart of London, yet for years, so many questions remained unanswered.

My intention in writing this book is not only to revisit the facts but to bring readers into the human side of the story—the joy before the darkness, the chaos of that night, and the resilience that followed. Every chapter is written with the utmost respect for the victims, survivors, and their families.

This is more than a tragedy; it is a story of accountability, justice, and the enduring quest for truth. If these pages make you stop and think—even for a moment—about the fragility of life and the importance of safety on our waters, then this book has served its purpose.

Thank you for choosing to read this story and allowing the voices of the Marchioness to echo once more.

Prologue

A Night on the Thames

Under the pale light of a moon in late summer, the Thames sat serenely, its surface mirroring the dispersed lights of London like shattered glass. The river was still safe for the odd splash, and a subtle wave murmured against the Marchioness's hull. While the metropolis slept above, pockets of life floated silently under the stars on the river. Subtle sounds of water lapping against moored barges, faint calls of nightingale, and faraway traffic hums blended together.

Antonio de Vasconcellos's birthday bash was a lively affair on board. A faint melody of jazz and pop floated through the night as glasses clinked and laughter grew in gentle waves. Drinks in hand, passengers meandered about the deck, swaying ever-so-slightly with the boat's delicate motion. Warm light from the cottage flowed over polished wood, glinting off brass railings.

Moonlight traced a silvery line over the river as a young guy leaned on the railing. His mind wandered lazily with the gentle swaying of the boat. Across the deck, friends toasted Antonio, lifting glasses in laughter. "Happy birthday, mate!" someone screamed over the music. The river seemed infinite, tranquil, and a shelter from the metropolis behind them.

Below deck, the crew moved smoothly. Captain Derek "Dave" Turner's eyes swept the horizon periodically, but there was nothing to see beyond the smooth sheen of the Thames. Deckhands checked bilge pumps, adjusted lights, and verified navigation signs were visible. One fresh deckhand gazed toward the river, noting a faraway shadow. He scowled, straining into the darkness, but Turner waved him off. "Just a barge, son. The water plays pranks at night."

Far upstream, the Bowbelle dredger moved with power. Captain Douglas Henderson stood on the bridge, gaze concentrated on the tight canal ahead. The enormous warship sliced through the water with a steady hum. The crew moved over the bridge, watching radar, adjusting engines, and scanning the river. One observer, binoculars lifted, spotted hazy objects on the banks, ignorant of the tiny, active sailboat downstream.

From Bowbelle's viewpoint, the Thames was ordered and predictable, guided by laws and routine. "Clear to starboard?" Henderson questioned. "All clear," came the reply, calm but ignorant of the Marchioness sinking below. Radar indicated only indistinct blips that disappeared in blind zones. The river's familiarity was deceiving; danger may approach stealthily.

On the Marchioness, passengers were blissfully oblivious. One guy saw a wave significantly greater than normal. "Probably just a fish," his pal joked. The birthday celebration kept on: toasts, jokes, and music. Moments of modest discomfort—a cool wind, a gently shaking deck, a tilted drink—passed undetected or were discarded.

The darkness in the distance lingered, extending down the river. The young guy at the railing leaned forward, peering. "Do you see that?" he muttered. His companion joked, waving off worry. Yet instinct prickled, unpleasant and obvious.

Minutes passed. The Marchioness drifted past moored barges. Laughter and music permeated the air. The shadow expanded, reaching strangely over the ocean. Passengers moved with easy elegance, leaning, drinking, and chatting. The crew fixed ropes and checked instruments. Bowbelle crept gently onward, unconscious of the little boat it was approaching.

The young guy at the railing leaned further over, eyes riveted on the shadow suddenly getting bigger. A cold raced down his spine. The reflection of city lights flickered anxiously across the sea. The buzz of faraway engines intensified.

The darkness expanded, taking more of the river in its mass. A threat unseen but coming, patient and inevitable…

Chapter 1

The Boats and Their Captains

The Thames spread like liquid silver under the late-summer moon, serene yet deceptively broad. At 1:00 a.m., the city was silent, its lights glistening in the water as if the river itself reflected London's pulse. Gentle waves murmured on the Marchioness's hull, breaching the surface just lightly. Distant traffic hummed softly, blending with sporadic screams of nighttime birds and the gentle slap of water against moored barges. On the river itself, life appeared nearly halted.

Onboard, the birthday celebration for Antonio de Vasconcellos pulsed with love and excitement. Passengers went around the deck, drinks in hand, laughter pouring freely. A portable speaker delivered light jazz and pop, mixing with the gentle swing of the vessel. Warm light from within the cabin streamed onto the terrace, reflecting off polished wood and metal railings. The mood was close, comfortable, and ignorant of what lurked upstream.

A passenger leaned on the railing, following the glittering line of moonlight across the lake. Thoughts wandered with the motion of the boat. Across the deck, a group toasted Antonio, their voices rising and falling, laughing flowing over with ease. "Happy birthday, mate!" someone yelled, their voice cutting momentarily over the music. The river seemed boundless, calm—a shelter from the metropolis behind them.

Below deck, Captain Derek "Dave" Turner moved with practiced precision. His eyes swept the horizon, yet the moonlit ocean provided little reason for fear. Deckhands examined navigation lights, tested bilge pumps, and made small modifications to keep the vessel stable. One fresh deckhand halted, observing a shadow in the distance. He grimaced and squinted. Captain Turner looked over, shaking his head. "Nothing to worry about. The water plays pranks at night." The young deckhand resumed his chores, unknowing that this shadow would blossom into calamity.

Far upstream, the Bowbelle dredger proceeded slowly, a gigantic presence slashing across the tranquil Thames. Captain Douglas Henderson stood on the bridge, gaze concentrated on the canal ahead. The warship, about 80 meters long, buzzed with authority, engines rattling through its steel structure. The crew moved over the bridge, checking radar, changing instruments, and keeping contact with the engine room. A lookout surveyed the darkness, spotting hazy objects along the riverside. None registered the little, cheerful boat downstream.

From Bowbelle's viewpoint, the river was ordered, predictable, and ruled by regularity. "Clear to starboard?" Henderson questioned. "All clear," was the reply. Radar reported just transient blips, vanishing into blind zones. The river's serenity created a false feeling of security. Henderson's team trusted routine; the night appeared predictable—but even familiarity might disguise danger.

On the Marchioness, people remained unaware. A guy saw a ripple greater than normal. "Probably just a fish," he added, chuckling gently. Conversations continued, music played, and the warmth of the celebration insulated them from uneasiness. Moments of discomfort—a cool wind, modest rocking of the deck, dropped drinks—were transient and disregarded.

Yet the shadow lingered, extending across the river in delicate, methodical motion. The passenger near the railing leaned forward, squinting. "Do you see that?" he muttered. His companion laughed, dismissing worry. Still, instinct stung, unpleasant and obvious.

Minutes passed. The Marchioness drifted past moored barges. Laughter and music stayed unabated. The shadow extended, crawling over the ocean. Passengers shuffled leisurely, leaning on rails, drinking beers, and laughing about the night's coolness. The crew walked between decks, fixing ropes, checking instruments, and keeping routine.

On the Bowbelle, the crew recorded normal observations. "Engine steady," one called. "Radar clear," another said. Henderson's eyes spanned the river, checking for impediments. The Marchioness remained unseen against the darkness—a little, fragile blip in a river that had no tolerance for the naïve.

The river itself looked impartial, a serene mirror containing both jubilation and imminent calamity. Currents altered little, undetected. Reflections from the moon rippled over the river. The darkness spread closer, almost palpable, rising bigger with every passing instant.

Back aboard the Marchioness, people continued to enjoy the celebration. A guy adjusted his coat against the cold, drinking whiskey. Another leaned over the railing, pointing at a distorted reflection. "That's odd..." he whispered. His buddies shrugged and laughed, ignorant of how carefully they were being observed from upstream.

On Bowbelle's bridge, Henderson's crew reviewed minor navigational modifications. One crew member noted a minor current variation but reported nothing else. Engines hummed steadily; the vessel pushed ahead like a quiet predator. No one regarded the little boat in their path.

Time slowed, stretched by stress undetected by those aboard the Marchioness. Shadows on the river deepened, the night whispering of activity. Passengers leaned on railings, their laughing a thin veil over worry. The crew worked swiftly, reacting to regular requests, oblivious to the rising closeness of the enormous dredger behind the shadow.

The passenger at the railing leaned more forward, eyes fixated on the black form suddenly growing across the river. A cold raced down his spine. Reflections from city lights danced anxiously over the surface. The murmur of faraway motors intensified, reverberating through the sea. The darkness approached persistently, patiently, and quietly.

Minutes became seconds. The two warships were now alarmingly close. On the deck, people remained unconscious, their attention busy with music, discussion, and transitory fears disregarded as insignificant. Below, the crew kept course, adjusting ropes and lights, oblivious to the threat looming quietly behind them.

The darkness grew, enveloping the river in its mass. The Marchioness drifted oblivious, caught in routine, laughing, and brightness. Bowbelle's steel hull drew gradually, inexorably closer, a quiet menace that no one onboard the party boat could yet notice.

The darkness expanded, taking more of the river in its mass. A threat unseen but coming, patient and inevitable…

Chapter 2

Down the River: Early Hours

The Thames at 1:30 a.m. flowed like liquid glass, its surface smooth beneath the moon's pale gaze. City lights shimmered on the water, expanding in extended reflections that flowed softly with the river's pulse. From the bow of the Marchioness, the river appeared limitless, a silvered ribbon bordered by darkness. The chilly night air conveyed a slight aroma of brine and oil, mixed with the warmth of spilled beverages and the faint smoke from a passing boat.

On deck, people laughed and joked, glasses lifted in repeated toasts. A group congregated around the cabin, swapping tales and mocking one another, oblivious to the night outside their tiny bubble of light and music. "I still can't believe Antonio is turning thirty," one commented, voice light with amusement. "Thirty? He's hardly grown up!" came the reply, laughter rippling across the deck.

The soothing swaying of the vessel lulled some into lying comfortably against the rails, viewing the reflections on the river, their minds wandering. One passenger adjusted his coat, gazing at the ocean. Something grabbed his eye—a short black line, a shadow against the moonlight—but when he blinked, it was gone. He shook his head and turned back, dismissing it as a trick of the mirrors.

Below deck, Captain Turner and his men kept routine. Navigation lights glimmered along the deck, and the hum of the engine resonated silently under the hull. Turner examined the water periodically, eyes alert for anything unexpected, but the river seemed empty and familiar. Deckhands operated methodically, ensuring the bilge pumps and ropes were in order, oblivious that upstream, the Bowbelle dredger progressed slowly.

Up the river, Captain Douglas Henderson studied his radar and charts on the bridge of the Bowbelle. The dredger hummed under its own weight, motors vibrating steadily through steel beams. Crew members went over the deck and bridge, calling out readings, changing lighting, and checking equipment. "Channel clear to port?" Henderson asked, voice calm. "All clear," a crewman said. The river ahead seemed empty, but the diminutive Marchioness glided undetected in the darkness, its tiny lights absorbed by the night.

Between 1:35 and 1:40 a.m., passengers' laughter floated over the deck, rising above the soft murmur of the ocean. Conversations flowed easily: jokes about spilled drinks, lighthearted taunting, and short concerns about the cold. Glasses clinked, some catching the moonlight in fleeting bursts of gold. One person leaned over the rail, pointing out a ripple in the water. "Did you see that?" he asked quietly. His companion shook his head. "Probably nothing. Just the current." They returned to their conversation, oblivious to the subtle movement upstream.

The river itself appeared peaceful, but small signals of strain arose. Reflections stretched and bent somewhat with passing currents. The murmur of faraway motors floated softly in the air. A quiet, low vibration went through the water under the hulls of both boats, unseen by most but registered faintly in the focused mind of the skipper. Eyewitnesses subsequently remembered these momentary moments—a ripple that appeared wrong, a shadow that lingered too long—but at the time, they were disregarded as tricks of the river.

By 1:42 a.m., the Bowbelle had come closer, its huge bulk cutting softly across the Thames. Henderson's team stayed concentrated on navigation, watching instruments and the river's minor fluctuations. One lookout leaned over the bridge railing, binoculars aloft, surveying the darkness. He noticed a flicker of lights far below, faint and distant, scarcely recognizable from the reflections on the sea. "Something down there," he mumbled. Henderson nodded but did not adjust direction. The modest lights were weak and impossible to identify, and in the darkness, the vessel ahead appeared no bigger than a buoy.

Passengers aboard the Marchioness stayed engrossed in discussion, their attention captured by the birthday party. Music, laughing, and the odd shout for Antonio hid the subtle warnings of the river. One guy observed a flicker in the water, a black line that extended momentarily in the moonlight. He mumbled a small, nervous remark, but his buddies chuckled and went back to the music.

By 1:45 a.m., anxiety grew incrementally. The Marchioness floated by another cluster of moored boats, reflections extending unnaturally down the river's surface. The buzz of the water appeared to grow, a vibration that ran softly through the deck, unseen by most but enough to stab at instinct. One traveler halted, listening to the gentle rhythms of the river. Something in the night seemed odd, a sensation of expectancy and discomfort, while the celebration proceeded oblivious.

Upstream, Bowbelle's shadow grew closer, quiet and huge. Henderson's crew stayed professional, focusing on readings, adjusting engines and lights, although the little ship moving below them remained unseen in the darkness. Radar indicated transient blips, impossible to decipher against the chaos of the river and reflections. The crew discussed small aspects of the current and river depth, unconscious of the coming collision.

And then, shortly before 1:46 a.m., the sound arrived: a quiet, almost imperceptible rumbling from behind. One person halted mid-conversation, glancing toward the stern. "Did anyone hear that?" he asked, voice barely above the music. Others laughed it off, but the tremor in the hull, mild at first, sent a shudder down his spine.

Something was arriving fast—something considerably greater than the Marchioness itself.

The darkness appeared to hold its breath. Laughter, discussion, and music filled the deck, but behind it all, a quiet menace pushed closer. Reflections on the river shimmered anxiously as the rumbling grew. Passengers sensed a faint disquiet, a short tingle of instinct—but the merriment continued.

The deep rumbling swelled, echoing through the hull, hinting of a tremendous presence coming rapidly…

Chapter 3

The Collision

1:46 a.m. The river shook. A deep, resonant rumbling filled the night. Glasses rattled. Music halted mid-note.

A passenger turned toward the stern. "What—?" The words died in his throat.

The darkness was upon them. Massive. Silent till now. The Bowbelle emerged out of darkness, steel, and size. There was no time.

Impact.

Wood splintered. Metal moaned. The Marchioness lurched violently. Drinks flew. Screams erupted.

"Hold on!" Captain Turner shouted. But the words were overwhelmed by smashing noises, water smacking frantically against the sides.

Passengers plummeted, clutching on rails. One guy crashed into another, both tumbling over the deck as the boat shook wildly. Shoes slid. Hands clutched thin air.

Below, Bowbelle's bridge was confused. Henderson yelled commands, voice harsh. "Engines, full stop! Stop! Stop!"

The crew scrambled. Radar displays flashed. "It appeared out of nowhere!" a lookout cried. Henderson's hands grabbed the console. The enormous dredger trembled.

Back aboard the Marchioness, anarchy ensued. A passenger lunged for the railing, but it tore loose under pressure. A woman's scream cut high. Someone yelled her name, but it was absorbed by the thunder of water. Cold struck first—sharp, frightening, difficult to ignore. Ice-cold water burst onto the deck, splashing, sweeping, and dragging.

Time fragmented. Seconds extended. Another passenger grasped a guardrail, eyes wide in shock. "It's tipping!" Another slid past, drenched, shrieking. Music and laughter—all gone. Only splashing, shouting, and the mechanical moan of broken wood.

From Bowbelle, the crew yelled warnings, smashed levers, and sought to balance the vessel. But the collision had happened. Henderson's stomach sank. The Marchioness was listing poorly.

A passenger fell into the river. Cold seized him instantaneously. Shock. Panic. Instinct. He struggled, striving to remain afloat, clutching at vanishing hands. Another grasped the first, tugging, but the current was brutal. Shadows engulfed them.

On deck, individuals slid into darkness. Screams and splashes reverberated off the sea, repeating and overlapping. The moon reflected only bits of bodies writhing, lost in the turmoil.

One deckhand clutched a shattered rail, eyes wide, teeth trembling. He attempted to approach another passenger, but a wave pushed them apart. Captain Turner's voice soared over the chaos, demanding, appealing. No one could hear him plainly.

From Bowbelle, Henderson spotted a human form in the sea. He leaned forward, binoculars wobbling in his hands. "Life jackets! Throw everything away!" The crew obeyed. Shouts carried over the river, but the Marchioness's mass moved forcefully.

Another passenger crashed against a hatch. Water poured in. Panic rose. Cold clawed at lungs. Clutching hands, desperate cries, broken wood under pressure. The boat's tilt intensified.

The river itself appeared alive, a cruel force consuming shouts, reflections, and corpses. The Marchioness listed considerably to starboard, then capsized nearly totally.

Time slowed again, but just for a second. Bodies clung, floated, and evaporated. The water swirled, cold and harsh. Life jackets bobbed. Flailing hands. Screaming voices. Darkness. Panic.

Henderson yelled instructions. The crew hurled ropes. Someone plunged into the water, only to be swept by the current. Onboard the dredger, terror was raw, abrupt, and instantaneous. They had hit a vessel. A party boat. A tiny, flimsy vessel. Chaos had come.

Above, shattered wood drifted. Shouts, gurgles, and water smacking drowned out reason. The celebration was gone. Music, laughing, everything. Only the water remained, engulfing, black, unending.

The Marchioness rolled entirely. Faces disappeared under the surface. Cold water claimed what the darkness had protected moments before.

The flood devoured them. Only flashes of terror appeared. Who would survive? No one could tell…

Chapter 4

Plunged into Darkness

Cold struck first. A jolt so quick it took breath and reason. The Thames, which had glimmered softly under moonlight moments before, suddenly seemed like a live wall of ice. One passenger, arms flailing, sought to reach the side of the upturned Marchioness. The wood was smooth, unyielding, and ephemeral. Panic rose.

Muffled shouts sounded from all directions. Voices overlapped: calls for friends, begs for rescue, sobbing, and breaths smothered by water. The river's current pulled at limbs unexpectedly. Some drifted, helpless; others struggled, teeth chattering, eyes wild, trying for anything solid to grab onto.

A guy remembers holding a railing, and suddenly it was gone, leaving only the cold to grab him. His coat, drenched, dragged him down. He kicked furiously, each effort sluggish and strained in the frigid water. Another passenger found a piece of floating lumber and clung to it, trembling furiously, mumbling prayers through chattering teeth. Eyewitnesses subsequently remembered the sense of shock, cold, and incredulity combining into one paralyzed instant.

Nearby, a small group gathered around a half-submerged lifeboat. Hands interlaced to keep each other firmly. One young guy, wet through, scoured the dark horizon, attempting to find friends or relatives. Every direction looked the same: dark water, shattered rubble, and frenzied limbs. A woman's scream ripped through the darkness, then gurgled into nothingness as she sank under the surface.

Heroism arose under turmoil. A passenger, stronger and taller, swam toward those struggling, throwing an arm or a lifebuoy when feasible. "Grab my hand! Grab it!" he shouted, voice strained and breaking. Others followed, creating cords of support among broken wood and floating goods. Eyewitnesses subsequently characterized this as instinctive and important—moments of lucidity under overpowering horror.

The river's surface was a battleground of disarray. Flailing hands clashed. Some were rescued; others disappeared under the sea before aid could reach them. Clothing and garbage intertwined, adding to the difficulties of mobility. Every breath was a battle. Every second, a recollection of warmth and joy is now replaced by the icy grasp of water.

One survivor, clinging to a floating chair, recalls the weight of shock crushing down. Time appeared to fracture: minutes stretched forever. Another victim recalled the experience of being invisible and isolated, asking for friends whose voices never replied. The Thames, a flowing, glittering road mere hours ago, was now an impassable pit.

The Bowbelle's crew hurried ropes, lifebuoys, and homemade flotation devices over the edge. Henderson's voice raised, commanding, encouraging calm, but the scope of the calamity overcame all attempts. The big dredger's lights sliced across the water, generating sharp rays that highlighted fear in fragments—shivering arms, shattered wood, and faces etched with horror.

A little hand gripped for a life jacket drifting past. A young guy grabbed for it, hanging on tight, as others struggled close. Every instant was a battle: cold water creeping into lungs, terror threatening to smother reason before the river could. Survivors recalled subsequently the difficult math of where to swim, what to grab, and who to save first.

Among the surviving, momentary heroism mixed with tragedy. A guy pulled a lady into a lifebuoy, but a current took him under. Someone else clutched to floating debris, tugging another on, only to witness a third go quietly. Muffled screams resonated in the gloom, accented by the odd splash or gurgling. Sensory overload—water everywhere, cold stinging, screaming mixing with shattered wood scraping over hull pieces.

Minutes went by like hours. The Thames marched ceaselessly, unchanged in its blackness, but taking the survivors inch by inch toward uncertain safety. The night air was dense with terror, the river conveying sound differently: distant voices looked muted, nearby cries keen and frantic. Every flail of an arm might signify survival or disappearance.

Then, in the distance, a gleam. A light—a little, wavering point—shone weakly on the horizon. A spark of optimism, but vague, remote, and fragile. A passenger pointed, voice cracking, "Over there… Do you see it?" Others tried to swim toward it, exhaustion and cold slowing them. For a moment, time halted. Rescue could arrive, or it might not.

The river remained cruel. Darkness still engulfed them. Others clung to people, others to rubble; some drifted alone, shivering, gasping, pulse beating. The gleam of light hinted at redemption; however, the result remained undetermined.

The Thames carried them ahead, cold, dark, and ruthless. The night had not yet finished, and survival still hung by a slender thread…

Chapter 5

Rescue and Chaos

Dawn was yet to come, but the Thames was alive with action. Lights from adjacent boats bounced over the lake, reflecting in fractured patterns on the surface. Police launches, fire personnel, and small private watercraft gathered on the site, sirens and shouting piercing through the residual darkness. The river, once calm, now held echoes of screaming, broken timber, and desperate appeals for aid.

Onboard a small rescue boat, Constable Graham observed the scene. "Keep your eyes open! We need survivors!" he barked, voice taut with urgency. Crewmen leaned over rails, stretching lifebuoys, ropes, and anything to capture floating corpses. Cold water sprayed over their legs, hands numb as they worked with frantic precision. Eyewitness testimonies subsequently recounted witnessing police and firemen rush into the river repeatedly, dragging weary, freezing survivors onto tiny boats.

A survivor grasped the edge of a launch, panting for oxygen, shaking uncontrollably. His clothing was drenched, and his hair was glued to his forehead. "My friends… my friends!" he shouted, eyes scouring the gloom. Nearby, another hand stretched from the sea. A rescuer grabbed it immediately, bringing the passenger onboard. The sensation of relief was short; more shouts filled the water.

The Bowbelle's crew continued to aid, dropping life rings and steering tiny boats closer to drifting survivors. Henderson's face was pallid, eyes wide with astonishment and responsibility. "Check the stern!" he screamed. "Everyone accounted for? Is everyone safe?" His group went slowly; however, the scope of the calamity made assurance impossible.

Amid the tumult, heroism became instinct. One fireman jumped repeatedly into the icy water, rescuing drifting passengers who clung to wood or one another. Each rescue was a battle: cold, weariness, and the unrelenting current conspired against them. Eyewitness stories subsequently emphasized the daring of those who risked their own lives, rushing into near-darkness to rescue others.

On the riverside, emergency workers coordinated. Stretchers were ready, blankets unfurled, and ambulances stood by, engines idling. Survivors were shuttled ashore, shivering, weeping, and in disbelief. Some grabbed onto pals, unable to accept that the trauma had ended; others scoured the water for lost loved ones, faces smeared with sorrow.

Despite heroics, delays aggravated disaster. The river's breadth hampered rescues. Debris and wrecks slowed progress. A rescuer cried, "Over here! Another one!" as he hauled a half-conscious passenger onto a launch. Behind him, another battle grabbed the eye: someone clutching hard to a damaged railing, almost lost to the river before rescue came.

Accounts vary. One survivor described grasping a lifebuoy, watching as desperate hands slid by him. Another recalled crawling across floating debris to reach a comrade, their combined weight threatening to capsize the rescue boat. Yet each instant was vital; every action counted.

From the boat, the river appeared alive with flight. Shouts, shouts, and splashing rang across the Thames. Rescuers dragged survivors from under shattered timber, carried them aboard boats, wrapped them with blankets, and soothed them through shaky voices. Heroism clashed with tiredness and cold. Every move, every second, held life or death in balance.

The extent of the calamity started to emerge. Bodies were pulled from the river, wrapped in blankets, and transferred discreetly aboard rescue boats. Medical personnel checked survivors on the beach, while police documented tales, capturing bits of recollection from people who had drifted in darkness for minutes that had seemed like hours. Statements would eventually build a mosaic of chaos: cries, splashes, heroic actions, failures, and incredible luck.

Henderson stared, mouth hard, as the Marchioness's corpses bounced in the water. The dredger had aided where feasible, but the sheer quantity of people, combined with the river's rapid current, had hampered the reaction. The whole enormity was just starting to become obvious.

As daybreak arrived, rescuers labored diligently. Every found corpse, every shivering survivor, contributed a piece to the growing tale. Some were living, others gone forever. The turmoil of the water left little assurance. Onlookers on the riverbank muttered in bewilderment, horror etched across their features.

The Thames had restored life to the coast, but only in shards. Some had survived; others had not. Heroism and tragedy entwined, leaving questions hanging in the early morning light. Who had survived, who had died—and why?

Chapter 6

Aftermath and Mourning

By daybreak, London awakened to a narrative too awful to ignore. News helicopters flew over the Thames, collecting shards of floating debris and tiny rescue boats. Headlines flew over newspapers and television screens: "Tragedy on the Thames: Party Boat Capsizes" and "Marchioness Disaster Claims Lives." Families, uninformed of the events until early reports trickled in, grabbed phones and phoned numbers anxiously, hoping for any news of loved ones.

On the riverside, survivors gathered beneath blankets, trembling, shivering, and looking into nothingness. A young guy revealed to a police officer how he had been clutching to a lifebuoy, watching companions fall under the waves. His voice shook as he spoke; the recollection was bright, vivid, and awful. "I… I don't know if anyone made it from my group," he muttered, eyes wide and empty.

Families started coming to the site, lured by news stories and a nagging worry. Mothers and dads searched the water, some crying aloud, others frozen in shock. A parent knelt at an empty area on the pier where a son should have come ashore. "Please… anyone… tell me," he implored, tears staining his cheeks. Media teams were relentless, microphones pressed forward, and cameras blazing, recording pain in raw, unedited detail.

Eyewitnesses talked to the media. One survivor reported drifting amid wreckage, grasping a friend's hand until the current ripped them away. Another recalled the chilly water, the terror, and the sense of being devoured by darkness. Their remarks were broken, interspersed by sobbing and stutters, but they formed a vivid vision of chaos and terror.

Hospitals received the rescued, cold and damp, some with hypothermia, others with minor injuries. Medical professionals labored diligently, their haste a juxtaposition to the silent sorrow creeping over families.

Blankets, towels, and warm beverages gave scant consolation against the emotional impact.

Onshore, tiny groups of survivors relied on one another. Hands clutched, heads lay on shoulders, and gazes were faraway and haunting. "I can't believe it... I can't believe they're gone," one whispered repeatedly, voice cracking. Friends and family members consoled each other as they coped with the immediacy of loss. Eyewitnesses subsequently characterized the riverside as a picture of grief: groupings of individuals tied together by tragedy, each bearing the weight of uncertainty and sadness.

Public astonishment went beyond the immediate families. Londoners halted their routines, watching news videos, reading reports, and trying to comprehend how a joyful night had turned into disaster. Calls for safety assessments and explanations mounted quickly; however, clear answers were sluggish to materialize. The Thames, once a symbol of leisure and enjoyment, now bore the imprint of abrupt loss.

Media crews swooped on survivors, demanding comments. Cameras and microphones entered vulnerable regions of grieving. One young lady recalled her adventure in the sea, voice shaky but resolute. "I kept thinking... if I let go... I'd never see anyone again," she continued, tears flowing. Another survivor stated, "People helped each other... but some... some we couldn't save."

Meanwhile, families gathered in homes, churches, and community centers, waiting for news. Volunteers gave blankets, tea, and assistance, although the emotional gap could not be filled. Mothers and dads, siblings and friends, clung to bits of hope, some clinging to the prospect that missing loved ones had lived, others silently lamenting the inevitable.

Even as emergency responders worked through the morning, concerns surfaced. How did this collision happen? Who held responsibility? Survivors' statements suggested bewilderment on both boats; however, no clear explanation surfaced quickly. Eyewitness evidence and media conjecture grew, piling pressure on authorities to act.

The melancholy atmosphere stretched beyond the riverbed. Parliament received calls from citizens expecting answers. Safety assessments of the Thames fleet were promised. Investigators started pulling together timeframes, navigation records, and witness testimony. The public's yearning for explanation and responsibility conflicted with the deep, unprocessed pain engulfing families.

The Thames had delivered its surviving and its dead. Families mourned. The media circled. The city battled with shock and sadness. And somewhere in the cloud of sadness, the first concerns of responsibility started to develop, silently but insistently…

Chapter 7

Investigations Begin

The morning following the accident, the River Thames remained littered with debris. Investigators from the Marine Accident Investigation Branch (MAIB) came, their faces set with determination. Cameras snapped, clipboards clicked open, and pens scraped on paper as formal processes started. The city watched attentively, and the families sought answers.

Captain Turner's logbook was the first document to be inspected. Times, locations, and notes were checked with survivor testimonies and Bowbelle crew statements. Investigators methodically recreated the timeline:1:30 a.m., Marchioness departed moorings; 1:42 a.m., Bowbelle proceeded downstream; 1:46 a.m., accident. Each second is evaluated under extreme scrutiny.

Eyewitness testimony presented vivid, often contradicting viewpoints. A passenger recalled the darkness, spotting the faint outline of a dredger too late to avoid. Another reported a silhouette on the lake shortly before the crash. From Bowbelle, a crewman said the Marchioness had emerged abruptly, nearly invisible in the dark ocean. Henderson himself testified to the limited visibility; however, concerns arose: why were radar and lookout measures insufficient?

The MAIB team noted procedural deficiencies. Lookouts had been designated; however, illumination conditions on both boats were inadequate. Safety standards existed on paper, although survivors and crew alike claimed confusion, preoccupation, and inattention. Investigators discovered gaps between records and eyewitness accounts: timestamps fluctuated slightly, activities varied, and important choices went unreported.

Investigators questioned survivors at makeshift receiving facilities. One lady recounted clinging to floating debris, hearing the Bowbelle's engines minutes before the crash. Her remarks, recorded precisely, stressed restricted visibility and a lack of warning indications. Another survivor stated that alcohol intake among passengers and party noise had concealed delicate aural indicators of an approaching vessel.

Bowbelle crew members were interviewed in turn. Some confessed they had not spotted the smaller craft until minutes before collision. Others highlighted the night's quiet, reflections on the sea, and fragmentary radar readings. Henderson stated that weariness and the repetitive nature of the river run may have contributed to delayed replies. Each revelation added weight to the growing picture: human mistake exacerbated by institutional inadequacies.

Meanwhile, experts investigated the accident scene. Splintered wood, bits of the party boat, and damage patterns revealed clues. Investigators noticed the Marchioness's lights were inadequately apparent for a vessel of Bowbelle's size at that distance and angle. The dredger's size and speed also had a key role in the accident. These physical features substantiated some eyewitness evidence while contradicting others, creating the contradiction between subjective experience and procedural truth.

MAIB investigators started producing a full report. Interviews were cross-referenced against records, radar data, and ambient circumstances. Investigators noted inadequate lookouts, poor illumination aboard the Marchioness, restricted sight from Bowbelle's bridge, and failures in navigation procedure. Legal counsel noted that although carelessness was clear, culpability remained a complicated question of maritime law and operational duty.

Media attention grew as early results leaked. Journalists reported survivors' tales alongside official declarations, showing the huge gap between actual experience and formal process. Families voiced displeasure at the sluggish speed of the probe, but officials advised patience, highlighting the careful nature of marine investigations.

As the inquiry proceeded, concerns of responsibility dominated conversations. Could improved training, adherence to procedure, or stronger monitoring have avoided the disaster? Survivor testimony claimed warnings were disregarded or overlooked. Crew testimony showed weariness and routine contributed.

Evidence pointed toward negligence—but who would eventually be held liable remained unclear.

The river had taken life, but now the investigation took attention. Logs, declarations, and rubble would speak in place of the deceased. The questions lingered: who failed in duty, and what penalties would follow?

Chapter 8

Trials and Legal Battles

Courtroom doors slid open under glaring fluorescent lights. Families, journalists, and interested bystanders crammed every available bench. The weight of sadness, rage, and expectation packed into the air. The trial of Captain Douglas Henderson had commenced. He sat stiff at the defense table, hands folded, eyes fixated on the floor, as counsel prepared to deliver arguments that may decide his professional fate—and, in the public view, assign guilt for a river that had swallowed many.

Eyewitnesses were called first. Survivors narrated the crash with voices shaking beneath the weight of recollection. "I saw the lights too late... we had no chance," one woman testified, tears streaming down her face. Another survivor, a young guy shaking as he talked, detailed the frenzied thrashing in the icy Thames and how he had witnessed comrades go under the waves. Each sentence accented with sobbing, each gesture a sad reminder of that night.

Henderson listened quietly, flinching at some testimonies, retaining control at others. His eyes briefly met the jurors' as attorneys stressed procedural flaws and irregularities on the Bowbelle and Marchioness. Evidence from the MAIB investigation was laid bare: inadequate lookouts, low visibility, and failures in navigation procedure. The prosecution's evidence created a picture of systemic failure exacerbated by human mistake, a disaster that could have been prevented with more attention.

The defense answered with points concerning human limits and environmental limitations. They noted typical river activities, darkness, and the suddenness of the tragedy. Henderson's attorneys contended that he had followed policy and responded as any captain would under comparable circumstances and that the mayhem could not have been averted totally. The courtroom held its collective breath as each argument was made, balancing anguish against legal precision.

Outside, the family waited with rising irritation. News crews hovered, microphones pressed forward, cameras blazing, catching anguish in sharp, naked detail. Mothers clasped palms to their lips, and dads paced, tears smearing their cheeks. "Justice delayed is justice denied," read one poster, hoisted high over the press. Public discussion roared: some demanded severe retribution, while others advocated forbearance, claiming that the river and human mistake were entwined in tragedy.

The jurors listened intently, taught to assess evidence with accuracy, but human emotion crept into the room. Witness testimony often conflicted: recollections distorted by fear, darkness, and water's tumult. Survivors' memories of distances, noises, and timings vary somewhat, allowing the defense space to raise reasonable doubt. Henderson's calm manner, however rehearsed, added weight to the idea that the calamity was neither purposeful nor entirely irresponsible.

Days went into weeks. Expert witnesses gave technical evidence: radar data, ship records, and marine safety standards. A navigation expert explained how restricted daylight and the river's reflections may have disguised the Marchioness until the dying minutes. Another expert studied Bowbelle's crew protocols, citing weariness and inadequate staffing as important problems. Each detail, each graph, and every chart heightened tension: the courtroom became a theater of pain, analysis, and moral inspection.

Families outside observed each day with rapt attention. They detailed the event to reporters, enduring misery as they awaited judgment. One mother remembered the moment she first received the news of the collision: "I couldn't breathe. My hands were shaking... I kept thinking, maybe it's a mistake. Maybe they're alive." Another parent reminisced about the rescue: "I saw men in the water, struggling... my daughter among them... I simply wished she'd be retrieved from the river."

Within the courtroom, survivors' testimony continued. A woman, who had floated for twenty minutes before being rescued, described the cold, the darkness, and the desperation that pressed against her chest like a physical weight. Her voice, shaking, drew many jurors to tears. Another survivor reported attempting to rescue a buddy, only to be carried apart by the river, the sight plaguing him now. Each piece blended the narrative of human tragedy over procedural analysis.

The culmination of the trial approaches with closing arguments. The prosecution begged the jury to assign culpability, underlining the avoidable nature of the incident. "Lives were lost not to fate, but to oversight," they stated, voices echoing in the anxious courtroom. The defense reacted with arguments about context, human limitation, and the fog of night, encouraging jurors to evaluate whether fault could be conclusively shown. Henderson's face remained calm, but a little twitch of the jaw indicated anxiety.

Finally, the jury returned. Everybody in the room held their breath as the foreperson read the decision. Acquittal. Henderson was cleared of gross negligence. Murmurs raced across the gallery—some sighs of relief, many of astonishment. Families grieved freely, some in astonished quiet, others in fierce fury. Outside, protestors yelled, journalists reported in real-time, and discussions raged: legal exoneration did not erase suffering, nor did it silence the public's desire for responsibility.

Eyewitnesses left the stand bereft, their terrible recollections apparently made inadequate by technicalities of law. Survivors returned to houses plagued by memories, knowing that although the judicial system had spoken, justice—at least in their eyes—remained unsolved.

The Thames had claimed its victims. The law had rendered its decision. Yet doubts lingered: if not Henderson, then who carried responsibility? The acquittal left an open wound in the city's conscience, laying the groundwork for a larger public probe into institutional failings, safety standards, and monitoring.

Chapter 9

Public Inquiry and Report

The public inquiry assembled in a majestic London hall, its high ceilings and polished wood echoing each somber syllable. Families of the dead, survivors, legal experts, maritime authorities, and media crowded the room. The air was heavy with expectation and anguish; every participant bore the weight of 51 lives lost on the Thames.

The investigation commenced with formal words from the presiding judge, stressing the necessity of openness and thoroughness. "This inquiry," he intoned, "aims to uncover the sequence of events, the causes of the disaster, and the measures necessary to prevent recurrence." Cameras snapped as relatives murmured, survivors fidgeted in their chairs, and journalists took precise notes.

Survivor testimonies were essential. One lady recalled the commotion immediately after the collision: the frigid water, the flailing hands of companions, and the effort to live against the stream. "I held onto him for as long as I could," she added, voice shaking. "And then... he was gone. Just gone." Another witness recalled drifting in darkness, hearing screams for aid that were never answered. Each narrative provided a vivid picture, merging personal anguish with methodological criticism.

Families recounted their pain, many falling into tears mid-statement. A mother told of the helplessness she felt waiting on the riverside. "I kept imagining every possibility," she added. "Each time the phone rang, my heart jumped. And then... silence." Others underlined the absence of quick warning, the lack of appropriate lookouts, and the inadequacy of river safety measures. Their sadness became witness to systemic failures.

Eyewitness testimonies were compared with official reports. MAIB findings were given in detail: inadequate illumination aboard the Marchioness, restricted visibility for Bowbelle's crew, breakdowns in lookout and communication procedures, and the cumulative impact of human error under stressful settings. Experts noted procedural deficiencies, emphasizing that although individual irresponsibility played a role, organizational shortcomings were equally essential.

The investigation investigated timeframes thoroughly. Every minute from 1:30 a.m. until the collision at 1:46 a.m. was studied, backed by logs, radar data, and survivor memories. Questions were raised concerning typical river procedures, crew training, vessel upkeep, and emergency readiness. Investigators studied whether drink, party noise, or diversions hampered the attention of Marchioness passengers and crew, while Bowbelle's tiredness and normal operations led to delayed responsiveness.

Public hearings featured comprehensive cross-examinations of crew members, nautical experts, and emergency personnel. Experts reviewed visibility constraints, navigation methods, and the mechanics of collision impact. The investigation blended technical analysis with human evidence, ensuring that every viewpoint, from procedural to personal, impacted the ultimate findings.

As the probe continued, comments on systemic problems became clear. Safety procedures existed on paper but were inconsistently executed. Training deficiencies, poor monitoring, and lack of established emergency protocols contributed to the disaster's severity. Witnesses reported how tiny mistakes, when coupled with environmental conditions and procedural deficiencies, spiraled into calamity.

Media coverage proceeded in parallel, magnifying public scrutiny. Newspapers published extensive analysis, survivor interviews, and extracts from inquiry procedures. Families and survivors were regularly called upon, their heroism both recognized and challenged by the public spotlight. Editorials discussed accountability: were they preventable errors, unavoidable accidents, or a mix of both?

Ultimately, the investigation issued recommendations aimed at averting future tragedies: greater illumination on passenger vessels, mandated lookouts and safety exercises, stronger licensing of party boats, improved communication methods, and documented emergency response plans for all Thames traffic. While these steps were praised, many questioned whether any process changes could totally remove human error and the capriciousness of accident.

The investigation finished with a thoughtful tone. Survivors and families were honored, their pain recognized as a cause for transformation. Maritime authorities acknowledged commitment to enacting safety measures, but investigators highlighted that responsibility stretched beyond any one person to the system as a whole.

Though safety measures were proposed, the shadow of the incident persisted. Lessons had been learned; however, doubts remained: could such a disaster really be prevented? Could the lives lost ever be recovered, or were they irrevocably engraved into the river's history? The public inquiry had spoken, yet the impact of the Marchioness accident would continue to reverberate.

Chapter 10

The Unanswered Questions

When the last decision was given and the Bowbelle returned to the shipyard where it would soon be torn up for scrap, many felt that the Marchioness case had finally been resolved. Official reports were written, investigation files preserved, and politicians proclaimed lessons learned. Yet for many who followed the case closely—and particularly for the families who lost someone that night—the explanations seemed insufficient. In fact, the farther one goes into the documents, the more frightening the image gets. There were gaps that refused to fill, facts that never felt right, and a lingering impression that the complete truth remained concealed somewhere under the chilly waters of the Thames.

Start with the warnings. Weeks before the accident, communications had been flying between river safety officials and operators regarding overcrowding on the Thames. There have been near misses between huge freight vessels and smaller pleasure boats, particularly during peak party season. Captains have highlighted worries about blind spots and the unavailability of suitable radar equipment for recreational boats. Yet despite these warnings, nothing changed. There were no urgent measures, no temporary traffic limitations on small portions of the river. And so, when the Bowbelle, a 1,475-ton sand dredger, drove into the Marchioness on that dark August night, it seemed almost inevitable to those who had been screaming the warning. But here is the question that nags at every facet of this tragedy: why were those warnings ignored? Was it bureaucratic inertia—or something more diabolical, a determined choice to choose business above lives?

Then there is the question of the Bowbelle itself. By all accounts, the vessel was a workhorse, making numerous journeys on the Thames transporting aggregate. But in the months before the crash, several crew members reported privately that the Bowbelle's bridge vision was hindered by her tall bow. Captains of identical boats have noticed blind spots so extreme that anything just in front of the bow may disappear from sight. This was not an undiscovered problem; it has been noted previously, even in earlier near-miss incidents. Yet government inquiries appeared unusually short on exploring whether the Bowbelle's design contributed to the accident. Was this omission an oversight—or a purposeful effort to shelter the dredging sector from expensive retrofitting regulations?

The chronology of the crash itself bears its own secrets. Witness testimonies disagree on the moments leading up to impact. Some survivors believe they noticed the Bowbelle coming down on them considerably earlier than the official timetable implies. Others report strange maneuvers by the Marchioness minutes before the catastrophe, as if its captain strove frantically to prevent calamity. Yet radar records reflect a different picture, one that neatly matches with the Bowbelle crew's statement. Were these differences the product of trauma-induced memory gaps—or was evidence deliberately interpreted to favor one story over another? Experts who have studied the investigation documents point out that some radar data was inadequate, and not all eyewitness statements were given equal weight.

Even the topic of alcohol consumption on both boats continues in debate. Investigators verified the presence of alcohol onboard the Marchioness, which was enjoying a boisterous birthday celebration. But how carefully was the Bowbelle team tested? Initial reports imply that blood alcohol readings were measured hours after the crash—hardly an instant measure. And when portions of those test data ultimately appeared, they were hidden deep in appendices rather than widely addressed in the final report. Why? Critics believe that the omission helped retain the impression of a reputable business operator, limiting responsibility.

There is also the disturbing subject of the crew's training. While official narratives highlight that both skippers were qualified, sources subsequently identified anomalies in how training records were managed. Some documentation looks incomplete, while others raise issues about whether specific safety exercises were even undertaken. If corners were cut, who permitted it—and why did the paper trail neatly fade at the edges?

The unsolved questions stretch beyond the night itself. Consider the salvage operation. In the turmoil of recovery, the wreckage of the Marchioness was lifted and investigated, but tales of what was found—or not found—remain frustratingly ambiguous. Some early divers reported severe hull damage conflicting with the stated angle of impact. Others pointed to structural problems that may have expedited the disaster. Yet these insights rarely arise in the inquiry's ultimate conclusions. Could important evidence have been ignored in the drive to clean the river and restore a feeling of normalcy? Or worse—could it have been surreptitiously disregarded to avoid incriminating regulators, producers, or operators?

Whispers of conspiracy may sound far-fetched, yet they continue. Families who spent years combing through documents describe a pattern: documents misplaced, responses delayed, and statements redacted. In one instance, a key safety memorandum circulated between government agencies just months before the disaster was "misfiled" and only resurfaced years later during a parliamentary review. Coincidence? Perhaps. But when set against the human cost—fifty-one lives lost—such coincidences become harder to comprehend.

The media, too, played its role in influencing what the people came to think. Early coverage focused on the party scene onboard the Marchioness, portraying an image of luxury and excess that some think inadvertently shifted responsibility onto the victims. Headlines highlighted champagne glasses and famous visitors, while devoting comparatively little attention to fundamental shortcomings on the river. Why this framing? Was it mere tabloid sensationalism—or a purposeful diversion from the corporate and governmental responsibility that lurked under the surface?

Even decades later, seasoned journalists concede there are flaws in the narrative—holes they were prohibited from probing into at the time. One former reporter remembers being "steered away" from questioning about the Bowbelle's maintenance record. Another was advised that pressing too hard on regulatory supervision may "burn bridges" with industry connections. These examples may not amount to evidence of a cover-up, but they emphasize a fact many families have long suspected: the complete narrative was never supposed to surface.

And then there are the personal stories—the families who still worry whether someone, somewhere, knows more than they've revealed. Parents who attended every hearing, only to leave believing that vital realities were left unaddressed. Survivors who relive the crash in their thoughts, plagued by the notion that what they witnessed contradicts what they were told. "They said it was an accident," one survivor recalled years later. "But when I look back, it feels like a chain of failures someone chose not to fix."

If the catastrophe was a sequence of failures, then where does that chain end? Was it with the Bowbelle's blind spot? The disregarded warnings? The lack of radar aboard the Marchioness? Or does it reach further—into boardrooms, where business considerations trumped safety measures; into offices where risk evaluations were filed away and forgotten; into legislative corridors where regulatory gaps were left conveniently open? The official story brings closure. But reality rarely does.

Perhaps the most disturbing enigma rests not in the technological facts, but in the quiet that followed. Silence from those who might have spoken louder. Silence from systems that should have secured life. Silence from a river that absorbed fifty-one lives and gave back only pieces of their dying moments.

Were these gaps in evidence just human error—or something purposely buried under the Thames? That question remains still, borne on the wave, waiting for an answer that may never arrive.

Chapter 11

The Voices We Almost Forgot

They were the first to arrive, and yet, in the ceaseless recounting of the catastrophe, their voices scarcely reverberated. When history is written, it remembers the dead, sometimes the surviving, and always the men in suits who sat in courtrooms creating the narrative. But what about the ones who stood knee-deep in the dark water of the Thames that night, feeling for corpses by touch because the searchlights were too dim and the current too strong? What about the men and women who held their breath as they dropped into a river that smelled of fuel and death?

One of them is Peter, a former diver now in his late sixties. His memory, however dulled by time, nonetheless sharpens with the mention of March 20,

1989. "I can still feel the weight of her," he adds, his voice shaking, not from age but from something deeper. "The first one I brought up. She was no older than my daughter. When I emerged, there was no sound on the boat. Just quiet. You never forget that type of silence." He swallows hard and looks away, toward the river that still flows cold and bleak.

For Peter and the other divers, the Thames became a cemetery that week. The river carried corpses far from where the Marchioness went down. Every time they dived, they hoped to discover someone alive, but on the second day, hope changed into recovery. "The water," Peter murmurs, "it clings to you. You fantasize about it for years." He acknowledges that the nightmares didn't end after the news teams departed. He consulted therapists who assured him it was normal—post-traumatic stress. But what is natural about retrieving the dead from the dark?

Then there were the emergency responders on the surface—the guys operating little rescue boats in pitch-black darkness and the paramedics waiting on the riverbank with blankets that never warmed anybody. Sarah was a young paramedic then, barely 23, recently trained. She had anticipated rescuing lives, not lining up dead beneath tarps. "You try to keep it together," she explains, "but when you unzip that first bag and you see a girl your age, you break. You simply break." She recalls how the media surged in, shooting shots and pushing microphones. No one asked her what it was like to embrace a parent who cried for a kid they would never see again.

The villagers, too, have their tales. Men who worked the docks, ladies who lived on the flats overlooking the river. They awakened to sirens and helicopters piercing across the night sky. For hours, they stood on balconies watching flashing blue lights dance on the lake. Some offered tea for rescues; others prayed silently, holding rosaries as the river swept secrets past their windows. "You don't forget a night like that," recalls Mary, who lived near Southwark Bridge. "We all thought, not here—not on our river. But then the names began pouring out, and it became ours. Our tragedy."

What unifies these lost voices is the weight of invisibility. And the probes started, and headlines shouted for justice; these men and women disappeared into the background. They were acknowledged in passing, their heroics squeezed into a word or two, overwhelmed by legal language and political platitudes. No one questioned how many of them drank too much in the months following, how many marriages collapsed under the strain, or how many now wake at 3 a.m. to the phantom sound of screaming over the river.

One former fireboat operator acknowledges that he quit the service two years later. "I couldn't go back on the river," he adds. "Every time I saw that stretch, I saw faces. I heard their voices." He stops, then continues gently, "Sometimes I think the river remembers too."

Even decades later, some meet silently on anniversaries. They stand beside the monument, its carved names glittering with rain, and lay flowers no one pictures. There are no cameras now, no headlines. Just the water, still carrying whispers. "We did what we could," Peter adds, voice quivering. "But the river... the river takes more than bodies. It steals bits of you."

And as the night falls and the water glints beneath the moon, some think they hear it—the faint echo of that night, the screams swallowed by the river, the final breaths that never reached the surface. It is the music that links them, the sound that will never leave them.

Chapter 12

Echoes Through Time

The Thames at night holds an underlying weight, its currents weaving history into ripples that appear almost alive. Lights from contemporary riverboats dance over the surface like restless ghosts, presenting an appearance of serenity that betrays the tales lurking deep below. For many Londoners, the Marchioness catastrophe seems like an event relegated to dusty archives, a name mentioned in passing or hidden away in an old newspaper headline. But for those who work by the river—or those who remember—it's a life wound that never really healed.

Today, London's South Bank is a kaleidoscope of laughter, music, and visitors capturing sunsets over the

Thames. The Millennium Bridge hums with footfall as elegant dinner ships glide by, offering an evening of luxury beneath the stars. Safety exercises are subtle but ever-present, and current laws impose tight operational standards. Yet when I question seasoned river workers about the night of August 20, 1989, there's usually a delay. They lean against rusty railings or the edges of polished decks, their gaze locked on the lake as if seeking for ghosts.

"Everything looks fine until it doesn't," says Graham, an experienced skipper who has spent thirty years on these seas. His voice is low, words laced with remembrance. "You trust the river, and then one night, it reminds you who's in charge. After the Marchioness, nothing felt the same. We received new safety guidelines, yes. Life jackets, lights, inspections—you name it. But the anxiety, the knowledge it might happen again—that never left."

The aftermath of the Marchioness accident compelled the industry to acknowledge its inadequacies. The adoption of required safety briefings, greater illumination, and the separation of freight and passenger routes were not merely bureaucratic tweaks—they were lifelines woven from anguish. Yet even today, rumors of complacency remain. In 2019, thirty years after the incident, stories arose asking whether contemporary cruise vessels would fare any better in a sudden collision. Technology has progressed, yet human error remains timeless. "Regulations are written in ink," says Graham, peering at the black river, "but the river doesn't read."

Beyond the practical changes, there's the issue of cultural memory—why certain calamities resound for centuries while others melt into quiet. In Britain, the titles *Hillsborough* and *Lockerbie* elicit communal fury and mourning vigils. The Marchioness, by comparison, appears to belong to a quieter, more mysterious kind of tragedy. Why? Perhaps because it occurred not in a stadium or a public plaza, but in the solitude of night, on water that absorbs sound and light both. The victims were young, lively, and part of London's creative heartbeat—and yet their tales felt half-remembered, like whispers floating through mist.

Dr. Eleanor Shaw, an urban historian I encounter at a café overlooking the river, gives her own viewpoint. "Cities curate memory selectively," she adds, swirling her tea with precise elegance. "The Marchioness was devastating, but it lacked a visual anchor—a burning wreck, a landmark collapse. It left behind pain, undoubtedly, but also uncertainty. And ambiguity evaporates rapidly in a city preoccupied with reinvention."

Yet for families who lost sons, daughters, and siblings, that uncertainty is awful. They struggled for decades—not for headlines, but for recognition. Some successes came late: the implementation of tougher river safety measures, the symbolic monuments that now stand beside the water, and the rare films revisiting that night. But recognition came at a cost. Years of public neglect seemed like a second tragedy, a creeping erasing of lives that mattered.

In chatting with river workers now, I perceive a duality: veneration for the past and acceptance that time dulls even the deepest scars. New generations of skippers remember the narrative of the Marchioness the way students know history dates—distant, sanitized. "We tell the newbies about it," one deckhand says. "But you can see it in their faces—it's just another rule to them. They don't smell the gasoline on the sea, and they don't hear the screams in the dark. How could they?"

As darkness falls into night, I wander the embankment, the river extending like a ribbon of ink under bridges glittering with light. The metropolis hums, untroubled. Somewhere beyond the brightness of the London Eye, a party boat cruises by, laughter ringing like bells. The river eats the sound, softens it into echoes. I wonder what it takes for a tragedy to stay alive in a city's spirit. Is it monuments engraved in stone? Annual vigils? Or the frail chain of tales transferred from one mouth to another, refusing silence?

Perhaps the Marchioness remains not in headlines but in quieter ways—in the reflex of a skipper double-checking his radar, in the silent shudder that passes through a diver when the water closes over his head, and in the moment a family stops by a bronze plaque and whispers a name to the river. Maybe memory is not about permanence but persistence—the act of remembering, again and again, even after the world has gone on.

And yet, standing there by the Thames, it's tough to escape the feeling that certain facts stay buried. Questions linger like shadows on the current: Did systematic neglect pave the door for disaster? Were warnings disregarded because profit spoke louder than caution? Official reports say lessons were learned, but the river doesn't write final chapters. It drags them onward, folding them into its depths, letting them emerge when least anticipated.

Fog starts to crawl down the lake, wrapping around the arches of Blackfriars Bridge. Lights flicker in the cloud, reflections twisting like shattered glass. For a moment, the city seems timeless—1989 and now combining in the silver-gray dusk. The river rushes on, quiet, uncaring, yet laden with echoes. Because the fact is this: no matter how many years pass, no matter how many skyscrapers grow along its banks, the Thames never forgets.

And neither should we.

"But the river never forgets—and neither should we."

Epilogue

The Night That Changed the River

The Thames glimmered under a pale moon, its surface calm, deceptively serene. Yet beneath that placid exterior lingered the memory of August 20, 1989—a night that had forever altered the river, the people who sailed upon it, and the families left behind.

Survivors walked its banks quietly, sometimes tracing the waters with eyes clouded by recollection. One woman recalled the flailing hands, the voices carried briefly on the current, and the cold that seemed to grip the soul itself. "Every time I pass this stretch of river," she whispered, "I hear them. I see them. I remember." Others spoke of the camaraderie that had arisen from tragedy: communities united in grief, advocacy, and the pursuit of safety reforms.

The disaster prompted sweeping changes. Navigation protocols were strengthened, emergency procedures formalized, and regulations for passenger vessels rigorously enforced. Lookouts became mandatory, lighting standards improved, and training for crews became intensive. Safety drills, once overlooked, were now an integral part of river life. The lessons were painful, born of loss, yet indelibly etched into maritime practice.

Families carried forward the legacy. They erected memorials, participated in commemorations, and shared stories to ensure the memory of their loved ones endured. Parents, siblings, and friends spoke of sorrow mingled with determination and of grief transformed into vigilance and advocacy. "We could not undo that night," one father said, "but we could make sure others would not suffer the same fate."

Cultural memory preserved the event in books, documentaries, and public discourse. The Marchioness disaster became a reference point in maritime studies, legal analysis, and civic safety planning. Its story served as a reminder of the fragile boundary between celebration and catastrophe, of human error compounded by systemic oversight.

And still, the Thames flows. Beneath the silver reflections of the moon, it carries echoes of laughter, terror, heroism, and loss. It reminds those who pass by of the lives claimed, the lessons learned, and the resilience of those who survived. The river is a living memorial, a silent witness to history, forever marking the night that changed it.

The water is calm now, but memory flows endlessly. The tragedy, the reforms, the stories of survival, and the echoes of grief all converge in that quiet current. And as the moonlight shimmers on the Thames, it whispers of lives lost and lessons learned—a haunting, eternal presence in the heart of the river.

Quick Memory Challenge

Congratulations! You've Reached the End... But the Story Lives On

You've just walked through one of the most haunting chapters in London's history. Thank you for staying with this story—every detail matters because every life mattered.

But before you close the book, let's make this experience interactive. Test your memory, challenge your perspective, and share your thoughts!

Quick Quiz: How Well Do You Remember the Story?

1. **How many people lost their lives in the Marchioness disaster?**

    - A) 45

- B) 51

- C) 58

- D) 63

2. **What was the name of the party boat involved in the collision?**

    - A) The Hurlingham

    - B) The Marchioness

    - C) The Princess Alice

    - D) The Empress

3. **What year did the tragedy occur?**

    - A) 1987

    - B) 1989

    - C) 1991

- D) 1993

4. **Who led the first major inquiry into the disaster?**

    - A) Lord Justice Clarke
    - B) Sir Bernard Ingham
    - C) Admiral Lord West
    - D) Lord Justice Taylor

5. **True or False:** The disaster immediately led to sweeping safety reforms on the Thames.

Do you believe the tragedy could have been prevented—or was it an inevitable consequence of a broken system?

Write your thoughts, share them with others, or even post online.

Your Challenge

If this story moved you, don't stop here:

✔ **Leave a review**—your voice keeps these stories alive.

✔ **Recommend it to a friend**—because history should never be forgotten.

✔ **Reflect on today's safety culture**—what lessons can we carry forward?

Printed in Dunstable, United Kingdom